leah

leah

Confessions of a First Runner-Up

SHANNON PRIMICERIO

TrueLife Bible Studies

TH1NK
P.O. Box 35001
Colorado Springs, Colorado 80935

TH1NK is an imprint of NavPress.
TH1NK and the TH1NK logo are registered trademarks of NavPress. Absence of ® in connection with marks of NavPress or other parties does not indicate an absence of registration of those marks.

ISBN13: 978-1-60006-112-7
ISBN10: 1-60006-112-5

Cover design by Charles Brock, The DesignWorks Group, Inc., www.thedesignworksgroup.com
Cover image by Istock
Creative Team: Nicci Hubert, Karen Lee-Thorp, Cara Iverson, Darla Hightower, Arvid Wallen,
    Kathy Guist

Published in association with the Books & Such Literary Agency, Janet Kobobel Grant, 52 Mission Circle, Suite 122, PMB 170, Santa Rosa, CA, 95409-5370, www.booksandsuch.biz.

Some of the anecdotal illustrations in this book are true to life and are included with the permission of the persons involved. All other illustrations are composites of real situations, and any resemblance to people living or dead is coincidental.

Printed in the United States of America

1 2 3 4 5 6 / 11 10 09 08 07

FOR A FREE CATALOG OF NAVPRESS BOOKS & BIBLE STUDIES, CALL 1-800-366-7788 (USA) OR 1-800-839-4769 (CANADA)

To Jessi Whitehead:
Thanks for always being a true friend.

CONTENTS

THE QUEST THAT UNITES US

EACH OF US WANTS TO be a star. Maybe not on the Hollywood big screen, but somehow and in some way, we want to shine. We want to be good at something. We want to be recognized. We want to be called out and chosen. Each of us wants to be *loved*. And in a fallen world, we don't always feel as if we are. Most of the time, that deep sense of love and acceptance we long for eludes us. So we chase it. With all of the effort we can muster, we strive to be the most beautiful, the most popular, the most athletic, the most scholarly, or the most whatever it is we really want to be.

Simply put, we compete. "Oh, I just have a competitive nature," we say. But really what our hearts are saying is, *I need to be the*_____ (best, prettiest, smartest, most popular, most athletic — fill in the blank as you see fit). *If I'm not, I will do my best to take out whoever is. My worth is wrapped up in this. Being second best won't do.*

More often than not, whatever we chase outruns us in the end.

Sure, for a time we may be able to catch up with our dream of being unconditionally loved and accepted — of being truly good at what it is we want to do — but then out of nowhere someone else steps into our lives, usurping our roles and snatching from us the titles we fought so hard for. But that's not the worst part of it. The worst part is that we think we're the only girl in the entire world who feels this way. We feel cheated and abandoned. We feel alone. Desperately alone.

And no matter how many times it has happened to us in the past, we always feel as if *this* time we will never be able to get back to that place where we had purpose and worth. We blew our last chance. As far as we're concerned, our lives are over. Well-meaning friends and family members usually use these moments to remind us that God loves us and thinks we're special.

We *know* God thinks we are special. Of course He does. He has to. He's God. We're His creation. He made us the way we are for a purpose, we've been told. Over and over again, we've been told that. Yet that purpose eludes us most of the time. One thing we have somehow missed in all of our moping is the fact that we are not *alone* in this. We aren't the first of God's daughters to deal with disappointment and discouragement. Our moments of insecurity and fear don't just unite us with God; they unite us with other girls — even girls who lived long before we ever arrived on this earth.

Insecurity is a language we all speak more fluently than we would like to admit. It spans generations and nationalities, hair colors and music preferences. Our low moments are what make us all the same at the core. How we deal with them, and how we use them for our benefit and God's glory, is what sets us apart.

The Bible contains chapters upon chapters telling the stories of girls just like us who wanted to be loved but seemed to fall short. They were girls who wanted to be somebody, somebody who mattered. In their lifetimes few of them achieved that, at least on the surface. Ironically it was after their deaths, as the pages of history were unfurled, that these girls left their marks. Let me mention just three.

One of them — Leah, the sister who was rarely loved and never chosen — became the mother of a nation that would forever be known as God's chosen people. Another — Hagar, the slave who was sent away to die in the wilderness because of Sarah's jealousy — became the mother of a nation whose political and spiritual unrest still marks our world today. And another still — Miriam, known mostly as the sidekick of her brothers Moses and Aaron — played a pivotal role in delivering the Israelites from the bondage of Egypt.

This Bible study is Leah's story. It's the story of the older sister who could never quite measure up to the younger. Overlooked and underestimated, Leah took her place with the rest of us in the Broken Hearts Club. But she didn't stay there. God lifted her out of her heartache and gave her a role to play in history that more than overshadowed that of the sister she couldn't seem to compete with. We'll see that God's providential hand took her where her strivings never could.

As we travel through her story together, we may at times find that peering into her story is almost like looking in a mirror. As Leah looked for love, begged for it, and even schemed and competed for it, her heart bore the same cry that ours do: *Pick me, pick me. Oh please, pick me.* Because of that, her story is worth reading. She was chosen by God even when the world rejected her. Her story will teach us the one thing we all so desperately need to learn: Life is not about being popular; it's about fulfilling our God-given destinies.

HOW TO GET THE MOST OUT OF THIS BIBLE STUDY

YOU HAVE A BUSY LIFE. Homework, sports, and other extra-curricular activities demand a lot of your time. I know that. To make this study easy to fit into your schedule, I have divided Leah's story into six weeklong segments. But I have not broken each week into daily assignments. It's up to you to find the easiest way for you to get through the material allotted for each week.

In order for you to get the most out of this study, it is vital that you take time to read the assigned passages. The main text for each week is provided for you, but you will be responsible for looking up additional passages on your own. It is also essential that you answer each question thoughtfully and thoroughly. The quizzes and various activities are fun, but they are also important. So don't skip over these portions, thinking you won't get anything out of them.

The ideal way to go through this Bible study is in a small group with some other girls so you can talk through Leah's story and the questions and issues that come up while exploring it. If you choose to do so, I recommend that you complete the assignments on your own each week and then get together to discuss what you have learned.

This Bible study can also be a tool to help you develop a regular quiet time with God each morning or evening. It's a great way to get into God's Word on a daily basis and study a girl whose life is completely relevant to your own. I suggest you set aside a specific time each day (like six thirty every morning, or eight o'clock every night) and commit to doing a portion of this study. That way, you will stay on track to finish studying Leah's story in six short weeks.

It is my prayer that through your study of Leah, you'll come to see and understand that God's Word is real and relevant to your life today.

Grace and peace,
Shannon Primicerio

week one

PALING IN COMPARISON

Leah had nice eyes, but Rachel was
stunningly beautiful. And it was Rachel
that Jacob loved.

— GENESIS 29:17

DO YOU EVER FEEL LIKE even your best isn't good enough?
Maybe for you it's not a beauty thing. Perhaps your sense of worth
gets snatched from you when someone gets a higher grade on an
assignment, or another girl on your team scores more points than
you do and wins MVP of the game. Or maybe it has to do with a
certain guy: Just when you think he is finally noticing you, someone else comes along and erases you from his memory. Perhaps your
experience — like Leah's — is a little closer to home and you have a
sibling you feel you cannot measure up to.

I felt like a princess the night of my senior prom. My hair and
makeup had been professionally done, and I had found *the* perfect
dress. But when I stepped out of the limo, my bubble burst. Not even
a yard away stood one of the most popular girls in school wearing
the exact same dress.

I could already hear how people would talk. *Hilary looks better in the dress than Shannon does. After all, Hilary does have a better figure.* I felt drawn into a state of mourning over my perfect dress that looked just a little more perfect on someone else.

Leah, the older of two sisters, lived back in biblical times. Her sister, Rachel, was "stunningly beautiful," but Leah's assets were not her looks. As a matter of fact, the Bible's first mention of Leah is a comparison between her and Rachel — and Rachel comes out on top. Some translations say Leah was unattractive or even outright ugly. Even *The Message*, which says it nicest, states that Leah wasn't nearly as beautiful as Rachel.

Although we may be shocked by this seemingly rude introduction to Leah, I suspect she was used to it. If her own insecurities weren't enough to convince her that she was not the favored, beautiful daughter, I'm sure the actions and words of others (including her father and sister) were enough to clue her in.

Stop and read the following passage, Genesis 29:1-20, so you have the proper context for this story before continuing. Pay special attention to how Leah is introduced.

Jacob set out again on his way to the people of the east. He noticed a well out in an open field with three flocks of sheep bedded down around it. This was the common well from which the flocks were watered. The stone over the mouth of the well was huge. When all the flocks were gathered, the shepherds would roll the stone from the well and water the sheep; then they would return the stone, covering the well.

Jacob said, "Hello friends. Where are you from?"

They said, "We're from Haran."

Jacob asked, "Do you know Laban son of Nahor?"

"We do."

"Are things well with him?" Jacob continued.

"Very well," they said. "And here is his daughter Rachel coming with the flock."

Jacob said, "There's a lot of daylight still left; it isn't time

to round up the sheep yet, is it? So why not water the flocks
and go back to grazing?"

"We can't," they said. "Not until all the shepherds get
here. It takes all of us to roll the stone from the well. Not
until then can we water the flocks."

While Jacob was in conversation with them, Rachel
came up with her father's sheep. She was the shepherd.
The moment Jacob spotted Rachel, daughter of Laban his
mother's brother, saw her arriving with his uncle Laban's
sheep, he went and single-handedly rolled the stone from
the mouth of the well and watered the sheep of his uncle
Laban. Then he kissed Rachel and broke into tears. He told
Rachel that he was related to her father, that he was Rebekah's
son. She ran and told her father. When Laban heard the
news — Jacob, his sister's son! — he ran out to meet him,
embraced and kissed him and brought him home. Jacob told
Laban the story of everything that had happened.

Laban said, "You're family! My flesh and blood!"

When Jacob had been with him for a month, Laban said,
"Just because you're my nephew, you shouldn't work for me
for nothing. Tell me what you want to be paid. What's a fair
wage?"

Now Laban had two daughters; Leah was the older and
Rachel the younger. Leah had nice eyes, but Rachel was stunningly beautiful. And it was Rachel that Jacob loved.

So Jacob answered, "I will work for you seven years for
your younger daughter Rachel."

"It is far better," said Laban, "that I give her to you than
marry her to some outsider. Yes. Stay here with me."

So Jacob worked seven years for Rachel. But it only
seemed like a few days, he loved her so much.

THE COMPETITION TRAP

1. How might have Leah felt growing up as the girl with "nice eyes" and having a sister who was "stunningly beautiful"?

   insecure, not good enough, self-conscious

2. What is the significance of introducing Leah to us like this?

   to give us a realistic idea of how others viewed Leah

3. Can you relate to Leah in this area? How so?

4. How does being compared to others affect you?

5. Are you ever guilty of comparing people to others you know? (For example, one parent to another parent, or one guy friend to another guy friend.) Explain.

Sometimes.

6. How can comparisons be destructive?

It sets people up for failure.

7. How can comparisons be beneficial?

It may urge us to "be better." (as comparing ourselves to Christ)

8. Was the comparison between Leah and Rachel destructive or beneficial? Explain.

destructive: it was based only on outward appearance.

OVERLOOKED AND UNLOVED

So here was Jacob, a strapping young man who went looking for a bride. He fell in love with Rachel at first sight — showed off a little at the well — and struck a deal with Laban (Leah and Rachel's dad) to work seven years for Rachel's hand in marriage. He loved her so much that the time flew by, and when the seven years had passed, Jacob went to Laban for his bride. It wasn't bad enough that Leah was the skipped-over sister the eligible bachelor didn't even notice; let's take a look at the scheme her dad put together. Look at Genesis 29:21-30:

> Then Jacob said to Laban, "Give me my wife; I've completed what we agreed I'd do. I'm ready to consummate my marriage." Laban invited everyone around and threw a big feast. At evening, though, he got his daughter Leah and brought her to the marriage bed, and Jacob slept with her. . . .
>
> Morning came: There was Leah in the marriage bed!
>
> Jacob confronted Laban, "What have you done to me? Didn't I work all this time for the hand of Rachel? Why did you cheat me?"
>
> "We don't do it that way in our country," said Laban. "We don't marry off the younger daughter before the older. Enjoy your week of honeymoon, and then we'll give you the other one also. But it will cost you another seven years of work."
>
> Jacob agreed. When he'd completed the honeymoon week, Laban gave him his daughter Rachel to be his wife. . . . Jacob then slept with her. And he loved Rachel more than Leah.

Wow! Imagine being Leah. The only way she got married was because her dad tricked some poor fool into doing it! And to make matters worse, when Jacob realized the error, he went flying out of bed to find Laban and see why he had been cheated. The end result was that Leah was sentenced to spend the rest of her life in her sister's shadow, as they shared the same husband. Even on her wedding day — when she should have felt like the ultimate princess — Leah didn't measure up. Can you relate?

Now, there are some cultural things we will have to overlook in this Bible study. Today, in the United States, it is not acceptable (legal) to be married to more than one person at one time. And it is also not acceptable (legal) to marry your relatives, as Jacob did (both women were Jacob's cousins, as Laban was the brother of Jacob's mother, Rebekah). Back in their time, both practices were not only allowed but also customary. So setting aside how weird this might seem to us, let's think about how Leah must have felt.

HOW WOULD YOU FEEL?

9. If you were Leah, how would you have felt when your dad took you to what was supposed to be your sister's marriage bed? Would you have enjoyed the wedding-night experience? Why or why not?

hurt by Jacob's reaction (maybe Leah had convinced herself that Jacob would change his mind about Rachel after being w/ Leah....)

if Leah was so insecure perhaps she knew Jacob wouldn't be happy but figured it was the best she could do given the circumstances ~ her only chance of being loved.

10. How would you have felt the morning after, when Jacob realized he'd been tricked and then ran off to find your dad, claiming he had been cheated?

ugly, not loved, not able to measure up.

NOT ALONE IN HER MISERY

Although our hearts break for Leah, we have to remember she was not alone in her misery. Imagine being Rachel and how she must have felt on what should have been *her* wedding day as her sister went off to honeymoon with the man she loved. Maybe at this point, Rachel thought that she would never be able to marry Jacob and that if she did marry him, she would always be wife number two.

Or imagine being Jacob—having worked seven years (that seemed like just a few days because of his great love for Rachel, according to Genesis 29:20) only to find that to be with Rachel he would also have to marry Leah, dividing his time between two wives. Although Leah's sense of self-worth was probably the most wounded in this situation, I'm sure a few others found themselves with broken hearts.

HOW DID THEY FEEL?

11. If you were Rachel, would you have been mad at Leah, or would you have felt sorry for her? Explain why.

    I'd like to say I'd feel sorry for her, but I think I really would have been mad.

12. What do you think Laban's motives were in doing this to Leah? Were they purely selfish? To what extent do you think he was looking out for Leah's best interest? Explain your reasoning.

    ✗ I think he didn't want to "be stuck" w/ Leah. Given the circumstances perhaps it also was looking out for Leah's best interest so she didn't become an "old maid" since a woman's worth in that time period was wrapped up in how many kids she had.

13. What about Jacob? How do you think he felt in all of this?

    He probably felt the whole thing was unfair but he sort of deserved it after all he had recently put his brother through.

14. Take a look at what the Bible says about marriage in Genesis 2:18-24 and what it says about lying in Colossians 3:9. How do you think God viewed Laban's plan to marry both of his daughters to one man?

The plans of man are not the plans of God. Sometimes we make the mistake of thinking that our plans are better or that we can fix a situation on our own. I'm sure God did not honor Laban's plans.

Although we may not be able to identify with being forced to marry someone our sister was practically engaged to, I'm sure we've all felt unwanted or like a third wheel at one time or another. As we continue to travel through Leah's story, we may not be able to relate to her exact circumstances, but we can all understand having relationships with imperfect people who cause us pain.

Leah's story is made up mostly of relationships — how she interacted with, and reacted to, other people. Your story consists of much of the same thing. How we react when we have been hurt says a lot about our character.

If your heart is broken, you'll find GOD right there;
   if you're kicked in the gut, he'll help you catch your breath.
     (Psalm 34:18)

WHAT ABOUT YOU?

15. How do you normally react when someone hurts you? Be honest.

> sad, hurt, upset — initially
>
> after that I really try to give it to God ~ not thinking about just me in the situation usually helps. (doesn't nec. excuse the other person, but it helps me to understand someone else's pain besides myself...)

16. Rewrite Psalm 34:18 in your own words, and explain how the knowledge of that verse can change the way you view your circumstances.

> Being broken brings us closer to God ~ as He is able to help us & we can feel His Presence.

GOD SEES WHAT WE THINK HE DOESN'T

Throughout Leah's painful story, we will find that God was with her. Even when circumstances were uncomfortable and her heart throbbed with pain, God was right there making something beautiful out of her life. Leah, the same girl whom Jacob passed by and Laban passed off, was the girl God chose to begin the lineage of the King of kings.

Back in biblical times, people were known by their lineage: who their father was, who their grandfather was, and even sometimes who their great-grandfather was.

Israel was eventually divided into twelve tribes — one for each of Jacob's sons. Jacob and Leah's son Judah was the head of the tribe that eventually produced King David and ultimately Jesus Christ. Leah's past may have been painful as she lived in Rachel's shadow, but her future was more than bright as God chose to send His Messiah — the Savior of the world — through her lineage. Oddly enough, the chosen son did *not* come from the chosen wife. Funny how God works sometimes.

He sees everything, including our heartaches and broken dreams. He sees the tears that fall when we think no one is looking. God overlooks nothing. And in moments when we feel the most rejected and passed over, we can count on His preparing a future that is brighter than we can imagine.

Our current circumstances may look bleak, but our future never is when we trust God through the hard times.

> You've kept track of my every toss and turn
> > through the sleepless nights,
> Each tear entered in your ledger,
> > each ache written in your book. (Psalm 56:8)

GETTING REAL

17. Do you feel as if God sees what is going on in your life? Why or why not? *Yes, I can rest secure that He has a plan for me.*

18. When you read about God seeing all of your tossing and turning, and of Him recording all your tears in His ledger, how does that affect your thoughts about a future to hope for?

It gives me hope that He will never forsake me.

WORDS TO LIVE BY

As we begin to understand how God really sees us and the magnitude of the destiny He has for us, one of my favorite verses comes to mind. Write it on a 3x5 card and tape it in your school binder or to your bathroom mirror. Read it over and over again until it sticks in your mind — and in your heart.

"I know what I'm doing. I have it all planned out — plans to take care of you, not abandon you, plans to give you the future you hope for.

"When you call on me, when you come and pray to me, I'll listen.

"When you come looking for me, you'll find me.

"Yes, when you get serious about finding me and want it more than anything else, I'll make sure you won't be disappointed." (Jeremiah 29:11-13)

PITY PARTIES VS. PURPOSE

Purpose is most likely something Leah didn't see in her life. After all, she never seemed to matter to anyone before. Perhaps you feel the same way. Maybe you wonder why you're here, or perhaps you're too busy feeling sorry for yourself to get around to questions like that. Or maybe you're too busy living to care about what you're living for.

Destiny. Does that word get your heart racing and your blood pumping? If it doesn't, it should. God has a destiny waiting for you that is wilder than any fairy tale and greater than you could ever imagine. Your life has the potential to impact others in a way that will shape their eternal destiny. Every day, or at least every week, you walk by people who are lost: at school, in the grocery store, at the mall. They don't know Christ, and they think God is some distant, gray-haired figure in the sky — if they even believe in Him at all.

[handwritten margin note: Worldly ← fairytales don't give God enough credit. His plan is bigger.]

Yet your smile and kind hello might be all it takes to soften their hearts and open a door for them to come to know about Jesus. But it's so much easier to have a pity party. It's easier to think about all of those people who don't notice us than it is to think about the people just dying for us to notice them. Don't you think it would have been easier for Leah to withhold love from the husband who never really loved her? Had Leah withheld love in its fullest marital expression, Judah never would have been born. Would the Messiah still have come? Yes, most certainly. But Leah would have missed out on being part of it — and Leah was God's first choice.

You are God's first choice. The eternal destiny of the world — and those in your world — is at stake. Have you noticed, or are you too busy having a pity party to care?

WHAT'S YOUR PPQ?

Here's a little quiz to test your PPQ — your Pity Party Quotient. Answer the following questions honestly, and then tally up your score to see where you stand.

A = Always, B = Sometimes, C = Never

1. When I feel as if someone overlooks me or something I have done, I tend to be in a bad mood for the rest of the day.

   A   B   C

2. When passing by others I don't know in the hallway at school, I am too busy to smile and say hello.

   A   B   C

3. If someone gives me a compliment, I tend to replay it in my head over and over again because it makes my day.

   A   B   C

4. When I wake up in the morning and look in the mirror, my eyes go directly to my flaws.

   A   B   C

5. One pimple is enough to put me in a bad mood.

   A   B   C

6. If I go to school wearing a cute outfit and one of my friends shows up in the very same outfit, I get angry and am embarrassed to be seen with her.

   A   B   C

7. If my crush asks someone else to the school dance, I lock myself in a bathroom stall crying.

   A   B   C

8. If I receive a bad grade on a test, I feel stupid and as if I will never amount to anything.

   A   B   C

9. If two of my friends pair up and seem to be getting really close, I feel left out and decide to stop speaking to them.

   A   B   C

10. If my sibling gets more attention from our parents than I do, I feel unloved and unwanted by my family.

    A   B   C

11. I base my self-worth on how I think other people view me.

    A   B   C

12. I treat other people exactly how they treat me — if they are nice, I am nice. If they are mean, I am mean. If they don't say hi, I don't say hi.

    A   B   C

13. When I am having a crisis and my friends are too busy to talk with me about it, I feel rejected and as if they don't care.

    A   B   C

14. When I read Bible verses about God thinking good thoughts toward His children, I don't think He could possibly think about *me* like that.

    A   B   C

15. I feel as if God doesn't hear my prayers about feeling unloved and rejected, because if He did, He would do something.

    A   B   C

    A answers = 1 point each

    B answers = 3 points each

    C answers = 10 points each

Now add up your answers and see what your PPQ is.

15–45 = Drama Queen. You are a walking pity party. The only time you are thinking about other people is when you are wondering what they are thinking about you! You are at risk of living a miserable life and missing out on your destiny. Spend some time reviewing your answers to see where you seem to struggle most, and work on those areas. Pray and ask God for eyes to see yourself as He sees you, and work on memorizing verses that may help. When you look in the mirror each morning, speak aloud to yourself and quote one of the verses you memorize—only make it personal ("I know the thoughts God thinks toward me . . .").

46–75 = Pity-Party Planner. You have good days and bad days, but you tend to spend a lot of time focused on negative things about yourself. Sometimes you make things a bigger deal than they really are. Next time you feel a pity party coming on, make a conscious effort to turn your thoughts toward the Lord instead of focusing on yourself. Memorize Jeremiah 29:11-13 and spend some time praying that the Lord would change your attitude and help you to see yourself as He sees you: as a precious treasure.

76–120 = Even-Keeled. You seem to have a good balance between throwing pity parties and knowing when to let things go. But even-keeled girls can have bad days too. Ask the Lord to help you continue to see yourself as He sees you. Memorize Jeremiah 29:11-13 so you are ready to ward off any pity party you feel coming on.

121–150 = Too Good to Be True? You answered almost every question perfectly, and you never seem to have a bad day or an insecure moment. Are you being honest, or just trying to look good? Ask the Lord to remind you of any recent bad days—or bad habits—and go back and retake the quiz to see if you get the same score.

TURNING IT AROUND

One of the most astounding things about Leah's story is that God chose to use her despite her flaws. She wasn't the prettiest or most popular sister, but her life had great impact. God could have used Rachel the way He used Leah, but He didn't. This was Leah's role to play in history. You have a role to play too. But you're going to have to take your feelings of insecurity, fear, and rejection and put them to work for your benefit. What do I mean?

I mean looking for others who may feel insecure or fearful and befriending them. I mean looking for your strengths and talents and putting them to use — after all, God made you good at those things for a reason. If you are tired of feeling as though you're not good enough, smart enough, athletic enough, or pretty enough, then stop sitting around having a pity party and make yourself available to God. Then He can change the way you view yourself and set His plans in motion for you to fulfill your destiny. Leah had to reach out and love someone who didn't love her back in order to fulfill her destiny. What do you have to do to fulfill yours?

THINKING IT OVER

19. Do you find it hard to love people who don't love you much or at all? If yes, why?

    Not anymore, but I did at one time in my life.

20. Think back to a time you felt insecure or fearful. How could you have turned that situation around, making it into something positive rather than having a pity party?

Talking It Out

Prayer is simply talking with God. If you're like me, it can be hard to concentrate for long periods of time when you pray. So try writing your prayer out. Ask the Lord to help you in areas where you may be weak, or thank Him for the plans He has for you and for making you who you are for a reason.

Writing It Down

Look back on what we have learned from Leah's story. What one point affected you the most? Spend some time writing about that point and why it stood out to you.

Setting a Higher Standard

The best way to get from where we are to where we want to be is to set a goal — to put something on paper that we will be accountable to actually do. In reviewing Leah's story and your PPQ, what is one area in your life where you need some work? Maybe you need to actively work at changing how you view yourself. Or maybe you need to try harder at helping others instead of feeling sorry for yourself. Whatever it is, write it down, date it, and check back in a week to see if you have made any progress. (And don't kick yourself if big changes take time!)

For example: "This week I am going to try to see myself as God sees me. The next time I encounter a disappointment, I am going to remind myself that God still has plans to give me a future to hope for and that I am not worthless."

week two

MAYBE THEY'LL LOVE ME NOW

Leah became pregnant and had a son.
She named him Reuben (Look-It's-a-
Boy!). "This is a sign," she said, "that
God has seen my misery; and a sign
that now my husband will love me."

— GENESIS 29:32

DO YOU EVER FEEL AS though you have to earn someone's love or respect? Maybe you try to get good grades in order to get a parent or teacher to notice you. Maybe you always have the latest new thing so your friends will want to hang out with you. Perhaps you feel pressure to be sexually active with a guy in order to have a boyfriend.

Whatever it is, I suspect Leah could have empathized. Having married a man who loved her sister, Leah found herself trapped in a one-way relationship. Her heart must have longed for Jacob to look at her the way he looked at Rachel, just once. Although Jacob never swept Leah off her feet, he was her only chance for happily-ever-after. Or so she thought. She most likely had no clue that God was creating His own version of her legacy. To gain the proper context for this week's study, please read the following passage, Genesis 29:31-35, before continuing.

When GOD realized that Leah was unloved, he opened her womb. But Rachel was barren. Leah became pregnant and had a son. She named him Reuben (Look-It's-a-Boy!). "This is a sign," she said, "that GOD has seen my misery; and a sign that now my husband will love me."

She became pregnant again and had another son. "GOD heard," she said, "that I was unloved and so he gave me this son also." She named this one Simeon (GOD-Heard). She became pregnant yet again — another son. She said, "Now maybe my husband will connect with me — I've given him three sons!" That's why she named him Levi (Connect). She became pregnant a final time and had a fourth son. She said, "This time I'll praise GOD." So she named him Judah (Praise-GOD). Then she stopped having children.

THE GOD WHO DOES

Last week we looked at how God really does see all that goes on in our lives. This week we will see Him doing something about it. The first sentence in this week's passage says so much with so few words. "When God realized Leah was unloved, He opened her womb." First, it tells us that Leah really was unloved and that it wasn't all in her head. Sometimes our emotions run wild and we can think things are true that aren't.

Many times when we feel insecure or fearful, those feelings are unfounded because we don't have all the facts. Someone once told me the letters of the word *fear* actually stand for **F**alse **E**vidence **A**ppearing **R**eal. Many times our fears are exactly that.

Back in Leah's day, the worth of a woman was determined by how many heirs (sons) she could produce. The more heirs she produced, the more valuable the wife. So God did what only God could. He made beautiful Rachel barren (unable to have children), while unloved Leah was fruitful. At the birth of her first son, Leah exclaimed, "GOD has seen my misery . . . now my husband will love me" (verse 32). Somehow Leah missed the point of what had just transpired. God *saw* — He saw that Leah was unloved. It says it right there in Scripture. And God *did* — God did something about it. He showed her favor and gave her a son. Yet all she could think about was Jacob — *maybe my husband will love me now.* Leah missed the amazing reality that God loved her — unconditionally, even when others didn't — and He was willing to move heaven and earth for her. Do you tend to be like Leah and overlook God's love?

TAKING IT ALL IN

1. Have you ever felt insecure or fearful, only to find out later that your feelings were unfounded? Explain what happened.

2. What precautions can you take to keep your emotions from going wild over something that exists only in your mind?

3. Why do you think we care so much about what other people think of us, yet treat God's love like it is unimportant?

LOOKING FOR LOVE IN ALL THE WRONG PLACES

The thing that astounds me most about Leah's statement in verse 32 is that she saw and acknowledged what God had done for her — she knew she had His favor. "God has seen my misery," she said. But it wasn't enough. She didn't overlook what God had done for her — she saw it. And she thought having God's favor was good, but she thought having Jacob's love would be even better.

But Leah's belief that Jacob would love her once she gave him a son proved to be incorrect. At the birth of her second son, Leah said, "GOD heard that I was unloved and so he gave me this son also" (verse 33). And at the birth of her third son, she said, "Now maybe my husband will connect with me — I've given him three sons" (verse 34). We don't know how much time passed between the birth of Leah's first son and her third, but it had to be at least a few years. Yet even as Leah produced three healthy heirs and Rachel sat childless, Jacob still loved Rachel more.

Leah had to come to the realization that she couldn't earn Jacob's love. Real love is unconditional, unrestrained. It isn't earned, and it is freely given. John 3:16-18 gives us a clear picture of unconditional love:

"This is how much God loved the world: He gave his Son, his one and only Son. And this is why: so that no one need be destroyed; by believing in him, anyone can have a whole and lasting life. God didn't go to all the trouble of sending his Son merely to point an accusing finger, telling the world how bad it was. He came to help, to put the world right again. Anyone who trusts in him is acquitted."

Romans 5:7-8 makes it even clearer that love cannot be earned:

We can understand someone dying for a person worth dying for, and we can understand how someone good and noble could inspire us to selfless sacrifice. But God put his love on the line for us by offering his Son in sacrificial death while we were of no use whatever to him.

No, real love cannot be earned. That would take everything real out of it. Love that puts itself on the line is a love that is not earned. It's love on our good days and love on our bad days. And it comes only from God. Yes, we are all called to imitate that kind of love toward others, but when we go looking for that kind of love, we can be certain of it only if its source is God Himself.

TAKING A CLOSER LOOK

   4. What have you done to try to earn someone's love?

5. How did it turn out?

6. Rewrite John 3:16 in your own words, but make it personal.
   (For example, "God loved me so much that He had Jesus Christ
   give His life for me.")

"Can a mother forget the infant at her breast,
   walk away from the baby she bore?
But even if mothers forget,
   I'd never forget you — never.
Look, I've written your names on the backs of my hands."
   (Isaiah 49:15-16)

7. Have you ever felt forgotten? Maybe it was your birthday and none of your friends remembered. Or perhaps everyone got together over the weekend and forgot to invite you. Explain your situation and how you felt.

8. What does it feel like to be remembered by someone you love? Think back to a time when a friend or family member remembered you — maybe they remembered a gift you said you wanted or they included you in something important. How did it make you feel? Why?

9. The Bible says that God will never forget us. How can Isaiah 49:15-16 comfort you next time you feel forgotten by someone you love?

FROM ACKNOWLEDGMENT TO PRAISE

With the birth of Leah's first three sons, she kept hoping to earn Jacob's love. By the time she had her fourth son, her perspective changed. Genesis 29:35 tells of her fourth pregnancy and the statement she made at that birth. "This time I'll praise GOD," she said, naming that son Judah. I don't think it was a coincidence that the son of praise became the son of the promised line.

The first three times, Leah *acknowledged* God and His role in the blessings she was receiving. But there was an apparent lack of praise, as her focus remained on Jacob. With the birth of Judah, her focus turned toward praising God. This change of focus was her launching pad to freedom. And although next week we will find that her attitude of praise was short-lived, it still illustrates an important point for us.

Many times we acknowledge God and the role He plays in our circumstances. But even in doing so, praise can be nothing more than a fleeting thought. When was the last time you sat down and truly praised God for who He is and not just acknowledged Him for what He's done?

TAKING A TIME-OUT

10. What are the main differences between acknowledging God and praising Him?

11. Do you tend to acknowledge God for the things He is doing in your life, or do you praise Him for who He is regardless of circumstances? Why do you think that is?

SHIFTING OUR FOCUS

12. We have countless reasons to praise God no matter what our circumstances. Here are six of those reasons and their corresponding Scripture references so you can look up what the Bible says about God for yourself. Reading the verses will help the reality of who God is sink into your heart and mind. Below each reason listed, write a statement of praise. I'll do the first one to help you get started:

Because He is my creator (Psalm 139:13).

Lord, I praise You and thank You for creating me and giving me life.

Because He is my heavenly Father (Ephesians 1:5).

Because He loves me (1 John 4:19).

Because He has forgiven me (1 John 1:9).

Because He gave me His Word (Hebrews 4:12).

Because He has a purpose for my life (Ephesians 2:10).

REFLECTING ON HIM

As I write this chapter, my grandfather (whom I am very close to) is in the hospital and for days has been in critical condition, unable to speak or respond to any of us. We are only ten days away from Christmas, and as I worked on compiling the list above, I was overwhelmed by another reason we can praise God. Matthew 1:23 says,

> Watch for this — a virgin will get pregnant and bear a son;
> They will name him Immanuel (Hebrew for "God is with us").

After I read those words, I had to turn away from my computer for a moment and cry. Yes, God *is* with us. And this Christmas I desperately needed the reminder. Not only is He with me at my computer screen, but He is also with my grandfather in the hospital and the rest of my family as we go through each day with heavy hearts.

Look back over the list again and think about the reminders you might need right now in your life.

13. As you read through the six reasons to praise God, which one touched you the most? Why?

14. What are some things about God that you tend to take for granted? Why do you think that is?

15. What can you do to remind yourself about that particular aspect of who God is?

A GOD-SHAPED HOLE

Many times, like Leah, we go searching for the love and acceptance of other people. What we don't realize is that other people are not capable of meeting our needs for love and acceptance. Even if Jacob had given Leah the love she so desperately craved, there would have been a part of her that still was not satisfied. A God-shaped hole exists inside each of our hearts.

Imagine the agony of Leah as she bore one son, thinking he would bring her love, only to realize it didn't work. Yet still she hoped, and another son came. And then another. The years went on, but Leah was still empty, unloved, and hurting. As she cared for each of her three sons, she was constantly reminded that even her best efforts could not make Jacob love her, nor could they fill that aching hole inside.

Then the fourth son came — and so did an attitude change. Leah began to praise God. The Bible never records her saying she was unloved again. However, it does tell us that her circumstances didn't change much. (We'll talk more about that next week.) The great thing about praising God is that even when our circumstances do not change, our attitudes and outlooks can. And when those change, everything changes, and suddenly we are not left empty — or unloved — anymore.

WHAT'S YOUR PERSPECTIVE?

16. What have you been focusing on lately: the God-shaped hole in your heart or God Himself? What's the evidence?

17. What are some things — or people — you tend to try to fill the hole in your heart with?

18. Describe a time in your life when your circumstances didn't change but your perspective did.

PERSPECTIVE CHANGERS WORTH MEMORIZING

I know we have covered a lot of verses, but it is important to commit at least one to memory as you ask the Lord to help you change your perspective and shift your focus from your circumstances to God Himself. Go back to question 13 and commit to memorizing the verse you selected in answer to that question. (Use the 3x5 card method we talked about last week — it works, I promise.)

POP QUIZ

Here is a test about the things we have discussed. Circle true or false.

1. I can earn the love of another person if I try my hardest and am constantly working at it.

   True   False

2. Acknowledging God and His work in my life is the same thing as praising Him for who He is.

   True   False

3. God may see the painful and frustrating circumstances in my life, but He doesn't *do* anything about them.

   True   False

4. Another person can satisfy all of my needs as long as I find the right individual.

   True   False

5. For my perspective on things to change, God must first change my circumstances.

   True   False

If you answered true to any of the questions, you didn't pass this quiz! Only a five out of five is a passing score, and all five answers were false. If you missed one of the questions, go back to that section and review what we learned about this week.

Leah's circumstances never really changed. Jacob's favoritism was even reflected in how he treated his sons: Rachel's sons were his favorites. But Leah bore the son in the chosen line. And when all was said and done, Leah's son Judah became Jacob's most fruitful seed. God's blessings, my friend, cannot be earned, just as love can't. But more often than not they are there, and we miss them because of our skewed perspective. Take some time to reevaluate your perspective before moving to the next lesson.

Talking It Out

Write out a prayer to God praising Him for who He is and asking Him to help you in any areas where you might be struggling. Remember, God sees and God does! So don't hesitate to ask Him.

Writing It Down

We have covered a lot of material, so please go back through the last several pages and find the point that touched you the most. Spend some time writing about what this new revelation (or old reminder) means to you.

Setting a Higher Standard

We could all use a little change of perspective. What area could you use a perspective change in? Write out a goal for what you want to change in the next week. (For instance, "This week I am going to stop trying so hard to fit in. I am going to remind myself that love is not something that can be earned, and I am going to look to God to meet my needs.") Remember to write today's date next to your goal so you can look back on it later and see how far you have come in a short time.

week three

COMPETING FOR THE CROWN

When Rachel realized that she wasn't having any children for Jacob, she became jealous of her sister.

— GENESIS 30:1

I'M SURE YOU KNOW FIRSTHAND just how competitive girls can be. The bad news is, it won't automatically stop when you get out of high school. Competition isn't something we outgrow with age; it's something we can overcome only with maturity. And it even dates all the way back to the pages of Genesis. It doesn't surprise me one bit that this cutthroat mentality among sisters is demonstrated in the very first pages of God's Word to us. Perhaps He thought this was one lesson it would do us good to learn sooner rather than later.

As we begin this week's lesson, please read the following passage, Genesis 30:1-13, to gain the proper context of Leah's battle with her sister, Rachel.

When Rachel realized that she wasn't having any children for Jacob, she became jealous of her sister. She told Jacob, "Give me sons or I'll die!"

Jacob got angry with Rachel and said, "Am I God? Am I the one who refused you babies?"

Rachel said, "Here's my maid Bilhah. Sleep with her. Let her substitute for me so I can have a child through her and build a family." So she gave him her maid Bilhah for a wife and Jacob slept with her. Bilhah became pregnant and gave Jacob a son.

Rachel said, "God took my side and vindicated me. He listened to me and gave me a son." She named him Dan (Vindication). Rachel's maid Bilhah became pregnant again and gave Jacob a second son. Rachel said, "I've been in an all-out fight with my sister — and I've won." So she named him Naphtali (Fight).

When Leah saw that she wasn't having any more children, she gave her maid Zilpah to Jacob for a wife. Zilpah had a son for Jacob. Leah said, "How fortunate!" and she named him Gad (Lucky). When Leah's maid Zilpah had a second son for Jacob, Leah said, "A happy day! The women will congratulate me in my happiness." So she named him Asher (Happy).

WHAT'S IN A NAME?

1. What do the names (and their meanings) that Rachel and Leah chose for their sons say about their own attitudes?

   a. Dan:

   b. Naphtali:

   c. Gad:

   d. Asher:

2. When the sisters gave their maids to Jacob as additional wives, what do you think their motives were? Explain your reasoning.

    a. Rachel: to have children – to be "better" than her sister

    b. Leah: to be loved by Jacob like Rachel was

3. Do you think giving Jacob two more wives was a good solution? Explain your answer.

    No – this was going outside God's plan for marriage. Plus, it was taking things out of God's plans for them.

4. How could Rachel have better handled her desire for children? How would she have benefited from this?

    She could have sought the Lord. (like Hannah)

5. How could Leah have better responded to Rachel's actions? How would she have benefited from this?

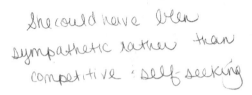

She could have been sympathetic rather than competitive : self seeking

THE HAVES AND THE HAVE-NOTS

Rachel was a girl who had everything. She was beautiful — and those of us who don't often feel beautiful can attest to the fact that the beautiful girls usually have everything else too. In this case, Rachel had the deep love and admiration of Jacob that Leah longed for. She had outward beauty that put other women to shame. It was more than likely that she was her father's favorite. But there was one thing her beauty couldn't buy her: children. Rachel was barren.

And even though Jacob defied the rules of his day and loved a wife who had given him no heirs, Rachel felt inferior for perhaps the first time in her life. Inferiority does something ugly to all of us who choose to give in to feelings of inadequacy. And Rachel got jealous. Jealousy does weird things to people too. More than anything else, it makes them competitive and ruthless.

Leah, however, was a have-not. Longing for love for probably her whole life, she always came in second place to her sister. Then God opened Leah's womb with one hand and closed Rachel's with the other. Suddenly, this girl who had lived her entire life in the land of have-nots had finally arrived. Leah had something Rachel didn't have — and wanted — so Leah held it in a death grip. She wasn't going to surrender the upper hand without a fight.

Frustrated with a God who wouldn't give her children, and

quarrelling with a husband whose love she was afraid of losing, Rachel took matters into her own hands and started a competition that wouldn't end until a great price had been paid.

We like to rationalize our motives.

At first Rachel's plan seemed to work. Bilhah bore a son named Dan. "God has heard me," Rachel cried, trying to hide her competitive spirit by making it seem as if she wanted a child for the sake of having a child and not for the sake of beating her sister. But when Naphtali was born, Rachel's honesty slipped out. "I've been in an all-out fight with my sister — and I've won," she proclaimed in verse 8, intensifying the war between two sisters.

WHAT WAS SHE THINKING?

6. Why do you think Rachel felt that having Jacob's love wasn't enough? What drove her to compete with her sister?

She always had it all — all of the attention & she thrived on this attention

7. Describe a time in your life when you had a lot of something (such as nice things, attention, or good grades) but it didn't feel like enough because of what someone else had. How did you react? What resulted from your efforts?

8. Do you feel the need to compete with others? Why or why not?

THE "ME" MENTALITY

Although it may seem that Leah was unwittingly forced into this competition with her sister, she was not entirely innocent, and she certainly didn't stay innocent. She began her adventure into motherhood with the wrong focus: She was focused on herself. And because she was so consumed with whether or not Jacob would ever love her, she delved deeper and deeper into a self-focused way of thinking.

When she saw the one area where she had gained an advantage over Rachel, Leah was not to be outdone. When Rachel began bearing Jacob sons through Bilhah's womb, fear gripped Leah's heart. Can't you almost hear her thinking, *But what about me? I'm supposed to be the wife with all the sons!*

Adding to the problem, Leah gave her maid to Jacob as his *fourth* wife. Thus, Jacob's first wife, who didn't like sharing him with one other woman, was now sharing him with three.

Competition can be hard to recognize. I don't enjoy competing with others and avoid it whenever possible. But there are still moments when I feel a competitive nature rising within me. For instance, when I get dressed to go to a friend's birthday party or another social event, I take extra time to make sure I walk in the door looking my very best. Part of me does this because I want to look nice. Another part of me does it so I am not outdone by any of the other girls there. When evaluating your own competitive nature, look hard and deep to make sure you don't get caught up in all of that.

9. If you are not a girl who gets caught up in competition, why do you think that is? How can other girls benefit from what you have learned?

10. After Leah saw that having four sons of her own wasn't going to make Jacob love her, why do you think she chose to compete with Rachel anyway?

She wanted to keep her "status."

11. Which sister would you tend to side with in this competition, or would you side with neither? Why?

Neither — I think their both wrong; never resolved initial conflict so it built up over time.

WHAT ABOUT YOU?

12. Today, marrying your sister's husband and competing over who can bear the most sons isn't really culturally relevant for those of us living in the United States. But most of us girls still compete over silly things when we let jealousy grow in our hearts. Think about the things you tend to compete with others over. Go down the following list and circle all items that apply. Remember to search hard and deep on this one before answering. Even if we are recovering competitors, that tendency to be the best usually still lurks somewhere in our hearts.

    a. Grades
    b. Attention from boys
    c. Attention from parents
    d. A place in the "in crowd"
    e. Awards and accolades
    f. Being the best on a sports team
    g. Other: _____

The reasons we choose to compete with others vary, and sometimes they can even be buried so deep beneath the surface that we have a difficult time describing why we do the things we do. But almost always our reasons for competing with others can be traced back to the way we feel about ourselves. Usually there is an area where we feel we don't measure up, so we need to take everyone else down in order to elevate ourselves. Or perhaps there is only one thing we feel good at, and if we relinquish our title of being the best at that, then we will feel worthless.

THINKING IT THROUGH

13. Be completely honest here. What are you most insecure about? And what makes you insecure about that?

14. How would you describe yourself to other people?

15. How do you *think* those who know you well would describe you to someone who's never met you?

16. How do you *wish* those who know you well would describe you to someone who's never met you?

17. When you compare the image of who you think you are with who you want to be, what is different between the two?

Who in the world do you think you are to second-guess God? Do you for one moment suppose any of us knows enough to call God into question? Clay doesn't talk back to the fingers that mold it, saying, "Why did you shape me like this?" Isn't it obvious that a potter has a perfect right to shape one lump of clay into a vase for holding flowers and another into a pot for cooking beans? (Romans 9:20-21)

18. Do you tend to feel like a vase used for holding flowers? If so, what are the benefits of being a vase?

which one are you?

19. Do you sometimes feel like a pot used for cooking beans? If so, what are the benefits of being a pot?

20. How does it make you feel when you realize that God made you the way He made you for a purpose?

21. What usually triggers your low moments in which you want to argue with God about the way He made you? (For example, getting a bad grade on a test, feeling left out by your friends, or not getting asked to the school dance.)

22. How can you deal with a low moment in the future?

POP QUIZ

How competitive are you really? Let's find out. Take the following quiz and add up your score at the end to get your results.

A = Always, B = Sometimes, C = Never

1. When one of your friends gets a cute new haircut, you feel the need to call your own hairdresser and make an appointment.

   A   B   C

2. After lunch at school you notice one of your friends touching up her makeup, and you suddenly feel the need to touch up yours too.

   A   B   C

3. When a girl in one of your classes mentions that she just spent $250 on a prom dress, you decide that you need to spend that much, or more, too.

   A   B   C

4. You accept a date with a guy you don't really like just because most of your friends are going out on a date on Friday night.

   A   B   C

5. When you come home from school and notice your sister's A+ test stuck to the front of the refrigerator, you decide to dominate the dinner conversation by telling your parents all of the great things going on in your life too.

   A   B   C

6. When shopping for new school clothes at the end of summer, you make sure you have at least two or three outfits that will really wow everyone who sees you those first few days of class.

   A   B   C

7. When you pull into the school parking lot, you do a quick survey of all of the other cars parked near yours to see how your wheels measure up.

   A   B   C

8. When you hear that your crush likes another girl, you immediately begin to compare yourself to her and nitpick her flaws.

   A   B   C

9. Once you discover the places where you have advantages over your crush's new interest, you begin to flaunt the areas where you come out ahead whenever he is around.

A   B   C

10. When SAT scores come in the mail, you immediately call your friends to see what they got.

A   B   C

A answers = 1 point each
B answers = 3 points each
C answers = 10 points each

Now add up your points and see how competitive you really are!

15–45 = Competition Queen. For you, absolutely everything is a competition. You are the type who likes to come out on top and is willing to go to any length to ensure that happens. When you are not winning, you are not happy. Sometimes your relationships suffer as a result of your competitive nature and people don't like to be around you. At the first hint of someone having something you don't, you begin to panic. Take some time to examine your heart and see what drives you to thrive on competition.

46–75 = First Runner-Up. Competition is a way of life for you, but you are used to not always coming in first place. At times you can be comfortable with being number two, but never any lower than that. And even then, the fact that you aren't number one still drives you crazy — although you would never admit it. The way you view competition is still unhealthy, and you should really spend some time focusing on who you are as a person, not where you rank in competition.

76–120 = Confident but Not Too Competitive. You can compete with the best of them, but you don't tend to thrive on it that much. Because you are aware of your gifts and talents, you want to make sure you are recognized for them, but you're not one to go after a title you know you don't deserve. Be careful. Girls in this category can easily fall into the trap of becoming competitive for the sake of being competitive if they don't watch it. Make a note to mentally check your motives and watch for an overly competitive spirit.

121–150 = Liar, Liar, Pants on Fire! The only way you could honestly get this score is if you never even look at other girls. Maybe it was the examples used in the questions that threw you off. But truly examine your heart, and make a note of the girls in your life who make you feel jealous and insecure. With them in mind, go back and retake the quiz and get your real score. Chances are you answered all of the questions in the way that you thought would give you the best score. When you got your score, did you want to check with all of your friends to see what *their* scores were?

REWRITING YOUR STORY

Think back to a time in your life when you were more competitive than you should have been. Go back to the place in your story where your competitive nature began to take over. In light of what you are learning from Leah and Rachel's experience, rewrite your ending with how you should have acted toward those you were competing against.

IS COMPETITION EVER OKAY?

In 1 Corinthians 9:24-27, the apostle Paul tells us,

> You've all been to the stadium and seen the athletes race. Everyone runs; one wins. Run to win. All good athletes train hard. They do it for a gold medal that tarnishes and fades. You're after one that's gold eternally.
>
> I don't know about you, but I'm running hard for the finish line. I'm giving it everything I've got. No sloppy living for me! I'm staying alert and in top condition. I'm not going to get caught napping, telling everyone else all about it and then missing out myself.

23. In this passage, Paul compares the Christian life to running a race. In this analogy, do you think we are competing against other Christians? Why or why not?

24. This passage can be seen as encouragement to run against our own flesh nature. If we truly run to win, we can overcome our own spiritual laziness. But many times we judge our own progress by comparing ourselves to others. What is the danger in that, and why is it wrong?

25. How can you run to win without competing against other Christians in the process?

WHAT OTHERS WILL THINK

In Genesis 30:13, after Leah's maid Zilpah had her second son, Leah proclaimed, "What joy is mine! The other women will consider me happy indeed!" (NLT). She was still concerned with what others would think of her: Would Jacob finally love her? Would the other women consider her happy even if she shared a husband with her beautiful sister? Her biggest problem was that she spent too much time focusing on other people and not enough time focusing on God.

26. Do you tend to be more concerned with what other people think of you than with what God thinks of you? Why or why not?

27. What are some things you are doing in your life right now simply because it wins you the approval of someone you desperately want approval from?

28. Has your concern for what others think of you led you outside of God's will for your life? Explain your answer.

Talking It Out

God says over and over again in His Word that He delights in helping us and will come to our aid whenever we ask. As you end this week's study, write out a prayer confessing your competitive nature and asking God to deliver you from it.

Setting a Higher Standard

What goal do you need to set to prevent yourself from falling into the same competitive trap that Leah and Rachel did? Set one new goal for yourself and put a date next to it so you can come back and check your progress.

week four

MANIPULATIVE TACTICS

Rachel said [to Leah], "All right. I'll
let [Jacob] sleep with you tonight in
exchange for your son's love-apples."

— GENESIS 30:15

HAVE YOU EVER WANTED SOMETHING so badly that you were blinded by your own want? As we dig into this week's lesson, we're going to see Rachel and Leah fall into that trap. Leah, who was still seeking Jacob's love, wanted one more night in which she could try to win him over. Rachel, who wasn't satisfied with her previous scheming, wanted a child from her own womb. Let's read Genesis 30:14-24 to gain the proper context for this week's lesson:

> One day during the wheat harvest Reuben found some man-drakes in the field and brought them home to his mother Leah. Rachel asked Leah, "Could I please have some of your son's mandrakes?"
>
> Leah said, "Wasn't it enough that you got my husband away from me? And now you also want my son's mandrakes?"

Rachel said, "All right. I'll let him sleep with you tonight in exchange for your son's love-apples."

When Jacob came home that evening from the fields, Leah was there to meet him: "Sleep with me tonight; I've bartered my son's mandrakes for a night with you." So he slept with her that night. God listened to Leah; she became pregnant and gave Jacob a fifth son. She said, "God rewarded me for giving my maid to my husband." She named him Issachar (Bartered). Leah became pregnant yet again and gave Jacob a sixth son, saying, "God has given me a great gift. This time my husband will honor me with gifts — I've given him six sons!" She named him Zebulun (Honor). Last of all she had a daughter and named her Dinah.

And then God remembered Rachel. God listened to her and opened her womb. She became pregnant and had a son. She said, "God has taken away my humiliation." She named him Joseph (Add), praying, "May GOD add yet another son to me."

TOUGH QUESTIONS

1. Why do you think God chose to answer Leah's prayer before answering Rachel's?

Rachel was selfish in not letting Leah be w/ Jacob, and she only shared because she wanted something in return.

2. How do you feel when it seems that everyone's prayers but yours are being answered?

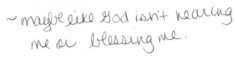

~ maybe like God isn't hearing me or blessing me.

Open up before GOD, keep nothing back;
  he'll do whatever needs to be done. (Psalm 37:5)

A LITTLE PERSPECTIVE

Before we can dissect what this passage fully means to us, we need to define an unfamiliar term and explain a few more cultural things that played into the unfolding of Leah's battle with Rachel. Mandrakes were apple-like fruit once believed to help women overcome infertility. Thus, Rachel wanted the mandrakes Reuben found so she could attempt to become pregnant and bear a child from her own womb rather than just that of her maid Bilhah.

And although both Leah and Rachel were legally Jacob's wives, for some unstated reason, Leah had lost her privileges as wife by this point and Rachel was the one who spent most evenings with Jacob. Thus, Leah had to barter with Rachel in order to have a night with Jacob.[1] After reading this story, I can't believe that some people claim the Bible is boring. This stuff is more exciting (and far more intense) than any TV show or movie I have ever seen.

---

1. William MacDonald, *Believer's Bible Commentary*, ed. Arthur L. Farstad (Nashville: Nelson, 1995), 65–66.

A CLOSER LOOK

3. In your opinion, were Rachel's actions manipulative or simply proactive? Explain your answer.

manipulative — she wanted it all Jacob & his kids (having)

4. If Leah knew that the mandrakes could potentially cause Rachel to become pregnant, why did she concede to letting Rachel have some?

she probably thought that she was more likely to get pregnant than Rachel was.

5. If you were Leah and you had given Jacob four sons from your own womb and two more from your maid's, how would it make you feel to know that he would rather spend his evenings with Rachel?

rejected, not good enough

6. Was Rachel's decision to barter a night with her husband for the mandrakes done out of love for him (wanting to give him a son), or was it done out of her own insecurity (feeling she needed to have a son to be worth anything as a wife)? Explain your answer.

   her own insecurity → she probably felt that Jacob was more hers than Leah's.

7. Make a list of the things each sister did right and wrong in this passage.

   <u>Leah</u>

   Right:

   <u>Rachel</u>

   Right:

   Wrong:

   Wrong:

8. Did both sisters have something to gain through this deal, or were all of the benefits one-sided? What makes you say that?

> *they both had something to gain ~~(text)~~ → the possibility of another child*

9. If there is something for both sides to gain, is it still manipulation? Why or why not?

> *Yes, their motives weren't right*

WORDS TO LIVE BY

Mean-spirited ambition isn't wisdom. Boasting that you are wise isn't wisdom. Twisting the truth to make yourselves sound wise isn't wisdom. It's the furthest thing from wisdom — it's animal cunning, devilish conniving. Whenever you're trying to look better than others or get the better of others, things fall apart and everyone ends up at the others' throats.

Real wisdom, God's wisdom, begins with a holy life and is characterized by getting along with others. It is gentle and reasonable, overflowing with mercy and blessings, not hot one day and cold the next, not two-faced. You can develop a healthy, robust community that lives right with God and enjoy its results *only* if you do the hard work of getting along with each other, treating each other with dignity and honor. (James 3:14-18)

SELF-EVALUATION

10. Have you ever manipulated someone for your own gain? If so, what did you do and what was the end result?

Yes → growing up w/ my sisters Even if I "won" it never felt good, I always felt guilty inside

11. Describe a time in your life when you were manipulated by someone you loved and trusted. How did that make you feel?

Love never gives up.
Love cares more for others than for self.
Love doesn't want what it doesn't have.
Love doesn't strut,
Doesn't have a swelled head,
Doesn't force itself on others,
Isn't always "me first,"
Doesn't fly off the handle,
Doesn't keep score of the sins of others,
Doesn't revel when others grovel,
Takes pleasure in the flowering of truth,
Puts up with anything,
Trusts God always,
Always looks for the best,
Never looks back,
But keeps going to the end.
Love never dies. (1 Corinthians 13:4-8)

12. What is the difference between manipulation and love?

they are opposites

13. Why is one so much easier than the other?

we naturally like to think of ourselves. Only christ helps us not to think of ourselves but others instead.

WRITING IT OUT

Write out words describing each attitude in the acrostics below. I have filled in some of the blanks for you.

Mean-spirited

A

N

I

P

Usually self-focused

L

A

T

I

V

E

Now try this one:

L

O

Very kind

I

N

G

THINKING IT THROUGH

14. How could Leah have safeguarded herself from giving in to
    Rachel's manipulative trade?

    She could have been content w/ what God had already given her.

15. In the personal example you used in question 10, how could
    you have accomplished what you wanted without manipulating
    someone else?

    *- stopped thinking of myself
    We live in an "it's all about me" culture*

16. How can you prevent yourself from being manipulative in the
    future?

    Christ-focused

17. In the other personal example you cited in question 11, what role did your insecurities play in your being manipulated by someone else?

18. How can you protect yourself from being manipulated in the future?

    Manipulation can come off as
    temptation...

WHAT'S IN A NAME?

It's interesting to see what both Leah and Rachel chose to name the sons who resulted from their manipulative scheming. Leah named her fifth son Issachar, which means "bartered." Her sixth son was named Zebulun, meaning "honor," because she thought Jacob would most certainly honor her with gifts for the many heirs she gave him. Rachel named her son Joseph, meaning "add," for she hoped God would add another son to her.

19. Explain what a name meaning "bartered" would signify to Leah. Why would she name her son that? (Hint: Think past the obvious answer that she had to barter with her sister to have a night with Jacob. There has to be something deeper.)

20. What does Leah's name choice for Zebulun (Honor) say about how she viewed her relationship with Jacob?

    She wanted to receive something from the relationship rather than always being "the giver"

21. The name Joseph (Add) implied that Rachel wasn't satisfied with just one son. Why do you think that was?

    wanting more . . .
    "the never satisfied attitude"

22. When you evaluate the name choices of both sisters, what motives for motherhood do you see?

    "all about me"

23. Think of something you desperately want. Do you really want to have it, or do you want it so you can earn love from someone else or take the lead over someone you have been competing with? Explain your answer. *or are you using someone you love to get something? think: sometimes we use people to get what we want. How do we make those people feel?*

GREEN WITH ENVY

One important thing to note in this battle of sisters is that each sister *coveted* what the other sister had. Leah wanted Jacob to love her the way he loved Rachel, and Rachel wanted a fruitful womb like Leah's. Coveting is a dangerous trap that we all tend to fall into easily. Simply put, both sisters were green with envy toward the other.

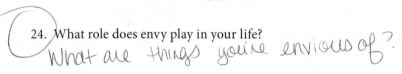

24. What role does envy play in your life?

What are things you're envious of?

25. Think back to a time when you were manipulative. What role did envy play in causing you to manipulate the other person(s)?

26. Is it possible to be manipulative without even realizing it? Explain your answer.

Yes, if you're only thinking of yourself.

THE KEY WORD

Don't be obsessed with getting more material things. Be relaxed with what you have. Since God assured us, "I'll never let you down, never walk off and leave you." (Hebrews 13:5)

I really love the way *The Message* defines coveting: lusting. The dictionary says that lust is an "intense or unrestrained" craving. That is so true. Anytime we are so overcome with our own wanting that we will do anything to satisfy it, we have become unrestrained. And manipulative people are definitely unrestrained. *think of a toddler throwing a tantrum*

Lust and coveting are never satisfied. By their very nature they always want more than they have. For them, there is never enough. And if we give in to either of these mentalities, there will never be enough for us either.

You're addicted to thrills? What an empty life!
The pursuit of pleasure is never satisfied. (Proverbs 21:17)

Another thing about lust and coveting is that it makes one overlook what she *does* possess in order to see what she *doesn't.* Leah had four strapping young sons before this manipulative encounter with Rachel. And Rachel had the unwavering love of her husband, even when she couldn't give him any heirs.

27. Why wasn't Leah satisfied in knowing that God had blessed her with many sons, especially when she saw that not everyone (such as Rachel) was so lucky?

She still didn't have what she really wanted: Jacob's love

28. What about Rachel? She had the unwavering love of her husband, even when she couldn't give him any heirs. Why wasn't she satisfied with this?

She wanted what she didn't have

29. Envy has a way of getting rid of any sense of gratitude we may have. Why is that?

We can't be thankful, when we want something we can't don't have.

30. Has the desire for what you don't have killed an attitude of gratefulness in your own life? If so, how?

31. List three things you should be thankful for that you usually take for granted:

    a.

    b.

    c.

ONE FINAL THOUGHT

In Genesis 30:23, when God opened Rachel's womb and finally gave her a son, she said something that gives us keen insight into her soul: "God has taken away my humiliation." Because her own humiliation over not being able to have children was so great, I wonder whether Rachel was even aware that she was manipulating and taking advantage of Leah. Too often, feeling bad about ourselves leads us to treat others badly.

Talking It Out

Write out a prayer to God asking for forgiveness for areas where you have been wrong, thanking Him for all He has given you (see question 31!), and asking for help in making the changes you need to make in your life.

Writing It Down

Wrap up this week's lesson by journaling about what God has taught you regarding the roles that manipulation, insecurity, ungratefulness, and envy play in your life.

Setting a Higher Standard

What do you need to do differently in your life and your relationships as a result of this week's lesson? List one specific goal for yourself. (For instance, "I am going to talk to my sister about how I feel inferior to her when she talks nonstop about her awards and accolades at the dinner table. I'm going to explain why I always seem to fight with her after this happens.")

week five

CHOSEN BY GOD

The family tree of Jesus Christ, David's son, Abraham's son: Abraham had Isaac, Isaac had Jacob, Jacob had Judah and his brothers.

— MATTHEW 1:1-2

HAVE YOU EVER FELT PASSED over or forgotten about as Leah did? I know I have. At the end of last week, we left Leah in the middle of a cutthroat competition with Rachel. As far as we know, she lived out the rest of their relationship that way. Genesis 35:18 tells us that Rachel died during the delivery of her second son, Benjamin. And although then Leah was Jacob's only wife (as Bilhah and Zilpah were considered concubines), his favoritism continued with his sons. I'm sure you have heard the story of Joseph, Rachel's firstborn son, and his coat of many colors.

Yes, Jacob favored the sons of Rachel over the sons of Leah, and again it seemed as if Leah was unloved and in the shadow of a sister she could never measure up to. But if we dig deeper into Leah's story, we will find that the wife Jacob never favored was the woman God did. It all started with a promise God made to Abraham, Jacob's grandfather, way back in the early pages of Genesis.

THE PROMISE

GOD told Abram: "Leave your country, your family, and your father's home for a land that I will show you.

I'll make you a great nation
 and bless you.
I'll make you famous;
 you'll be a blessing.
I'll bless those who bless you;
 those who curse you I'll curse.
All the families of the Earth
 will be blessed through you." (Genesis 12:1-3)

That, right there, was God's promise that He would send the Messiah through the line of Abraham. And although generations and generations passed between the time of Abraham and the time of Jesus Christ, God was true to His word. Judah was part of the ful-fillment of that promise, and Judah was Leah's son.

The family tree of Jesus Christ, David's son, Abraham's son:

Abraham had Isaac,
Isaac had Jacob,
Jacob had Judah and his brothers. (Matthew 1:1-2)

For the first time in perhaps ever, Leah's son was mentioned in a positive light and Rachel's sons were only briefly referenced as "Judah's brothers." The son who Leah named "Praise-GOD" (Genesis 29:35), the only son whom she didn't view as a tool with which she could win Jacob's affection, the son whose DNA was half hers and not Rachel's, was the son God used to help fulfill the promise of the coming Messiah. Simply put, Leah was a great-great-(many greats)-grandmother of Jesus Christ Himself.

1. God blessed Leah in this radical way but never let her see it in her lifetime. How do you feel about this kind of blessing? Why?

   It involves having faith.

2. What role, if any, did humility play in Leah's life?

POP QUIZ

Sometimes false humility can masquerade as the real thing. Because it is important that those of us who are Christians learn the difference between the two, take this quiz and see how well you can distinguish between them. Write an "H" next to all of the sentences describing humility, and an "F" next to all of the sentences describing false humility.

1. Has a low self-image and thinks very poorly of herself. _____

2. Makes sure to mention that God gave her the talents she has but proceeds to talk nonstop about herself. _____

3. Talks badly about herself and downplays any compliment anyone gives her. _____

4. Is always striving to be humble by making sure that everyone knows she doesn't think too highly of herself. _____

5. Makes sure to compliment others when she really doesn't mean it just so people won't think she's arrogant. _____

6. Says things about herself that she knows aren't true. (For instance, "No, I'm really not any good at playing soccer. I don't even know why they keep me on the team.") _____

7. Purposely messes up at something she is good at so people won't think she believes she is the best. _____

The correct answer to all of the statements is "F": false humility. A lot of people have a distorted idea of what humility is. Humility *isn't* thinking poorly of yourself. It *isn't* having a pity party. In fact, real humility doesn't even involve thinking about yourself at all. Humility *is* recognizing God as King of kings and Lord of lords and being awed that He chooses to love you and use you. What most people don't realize is that false humility is really pride in disguise because it is all self-focused, whereas true humility is God-focused.

3. Which of the statements on the quiz is the hardest for you to accept as being false? Why?

4. From what you know of Leah's life, was she someone you would classify as truly humble or falsely humble? Why?

 falsely humble

5. What about you? Are you truly humble? (This could be seen as a trick question. Do humble people know they are humble?)

WHY DID GOD CHOOSE HER?

6. Was Rachel any more or less humble than Leah? Explain.

7. What role do you think Leah's rejection by men played in preparing her to be chosen by God?

She couldn't rely on a man in life to provide for her needs. Rather, she had to rely on God for fulfillment.

* Who or what fulfills you?

Is there anyone around who can explain God?
Anyone smart enough to tell Him what to do?
Anyone who has done ~~Him such a~~ huge favor that God has
to ask his advice? (Romans 11:34-35)

8. It may be hard for you to understand why God chose to use
   Leah to play such an important role in history. Do you ever feel
   the same way about yourself? Explain.

Be honest! List the top 5 things that you think about during the course of the day.

9. List five things you would love to do with your life that you
   think are beyond the scope of what God would do in and
   through you.

   a.

   b.

   c.

   d.

   e.

10. Why do you believe that God would never do those things in
    you, through you, or for you?

You don't have this list to share with the ones that don't glorify God. Pray about those things & replacing them w/ more God-glorifying desires. There's a big world out there — out of the box of ourselves that God can't use in that He doesn't ask perfect. He asks that we come submit to HIS will

98

11. Look up the verses listed next to the following people who played major roles in God's story. In the space next to their name, make a note of any of the characteristics mentioned about their appearance, personality, or loyalty.

   a. Paul — an apostle, a key player in the early church, and the writer of much of the New Testament (2 Corinthians 12:1-10)

   b. Jeremiah — a prophet who remained faithful to God in a generation of people who went astray (Jeremiah 1:6-9)

   c. Moses — the key figure God used to deliver the people of Israel from slavery in Egypt (Exodus 4:10-17)

   d. Mary — the young virgin who became the mother of Christ (Luke 1:26-38)

e. Peter — one of Jesus' twelve disciples, one of Jesus' three closest friends, a key player in the early church (Luke 22:54-62)

12. Review the list in question 11. Would those people be the ones you would have chosen for their special tasks? Why or why not?

13. Yet God still chose to use every single one of them when He could have easily chosen someone else. Why do you think that is?

14. Reread Genesis 29:1–30:24 (Leah's story). Make a list of Leah's mistakes.

15. If God does not choose people based on their own merit, what does He base His choices on?

16. Describe a time in your own life when you felt as if God could never love you or use you and He proved you wrong.

17. Describe a time when you met, read, or heard about someone you never thought God could love or use, yet He did. What do you remember feeling when you heard this story?

There's nobody living right, not even one,
  nobody who knows the score, nobody alert for God.
They've all taken the wrong turn;
  they've all wandered down blind alleys.
No one's living right;
  I can't find a single one.
Their throats are gaping graves,
  their tongues slick as mud slides.
Every word they speak is tinged with poison.
  They open their mouths and pollute the air.
They race for the honor of sinner-of-the-year,
  litter the land with heartbreak and ruin,
Don't know the first thing about living with others.
  They never give God the time of day. (Romans 3:10-18)

18. How does reading the Romans passage make you feel?

inferior, gives a sense of urgency

"This is how much God loved the world: He gave his Son, his one and only Son. And this is why: so that no one need be destroyed; by believing in him, anyone can have a whole and lasting life. God didn't go to all the trouble of sending his Son merely to point an accusing finger, telling the world how bad it was. He came to help, to put the world right again." (John 3:16-17)

19. How does reading that passage make you feel? Why?

gives hope, makes me want to give a little back to God

LET'S REVIEW

20. It may seem unfair that God did something great for Leah that she never saw this side of heaven. But let's review all that God did for Leah in her lifetime that she may not have noticed at first glance. Look up the following verses and write down the blessing God gave Leah in each verse.

Genesis 29:32

Genesis 29:33

Genesis 29:34

Genesis 29:35

Genesis 30:17

Genesis 30:19

Genesis 30:21

God gave Leah seven healthy children, whereas Rachel was given only two and died before she could watch them grow up. Even though Leah didn't know about the legacy God was building through her son Judah, surely she knew that He had made her fruitful and blessed. Yet we never even once see her acknowledge that in Scripture.

21. Why do you think Leah never acknowledged what a blessing it was to have seven children? (Note: She did acknowledge it in the context of how much her husband should love her for bearing so many sons, but why didn't she acknowledge it outside of that context?)

A ROLE TO PLAY IN GOD'S STORY

Just as Leah had a specific role to play in God's story, one that no one else — not even beautiful Rachel — could fill, you have a role that is your own to play in God's story. Leah's role was to be the mother of

Judah and pass on the family line. Your role more than likely involves the timing and placement of where you live and go to school during this very moment.

> [God] made from one man every nation of mankind to live on all the face of the earth, having determined their appointed times and the boundaries of their habitation. (Acts 17:26, NASB)

22. In one or two paragraphs, describe your current situation (where you live, where you go to school, who you live with, who you go to school with, and so on).

23. Make a list of unsaved people or unsaved groups of people you come in contact with on a regular basis. They could be unsaved family members, kids at school, or salespeople in the mall where you hang out. Think creatively here.

1.   6.

2.   7.

3.   8.

4.   9.

5.   10.

24. Make a list of the tools God has given you to tell His story to others. (These can be areas where you are gifted, such as art, sports, or music. They can be passions you have, like working with children or elderly people.)

1.   6.

2.   7.

3.   8.

4.   9.

5.   10.

25. Describe your involvement with your current youth group.

26. Are there any outreach opportunities through your youth group that you do or don't take advantage of? What are they? (Think of mission trips, community volunteer work, youth camps you could invite people to, and so on.)

27. Evaluate your last five answers. Can you catch even the smallest glimpse of what your role to play in God's story may be at this moment? If so, what is it?

28. If you're still having a hard time figuring out what your role to play in God's story might be at this time, make a list of three (Christian) people (at least one adult) who can help you evaluate your answers to questions 22–26 and who will pray with you as you seek God's will.

    1.

    2.

    3.

WRAPPING IT UP

Leah missed her glimpse into the role God wanted her to play in history. Sure, she may never have been able to guess that the Messiah would come from her lineage, but a fruitful womb was a pretty good indication that God was going to use motherhood in a special way in her life. Not many women have seven children, even in her day.

Make sure you don't overlook the hints and glimpses God is giving you into His purpose for your life. If we can learn anything from Leah's story this week, it is that there is more to each of us than meets the eye. Look deeper into your life and what God is doing there. Don't miss the opportunities He is giving you. Don't waste another minute!

I won my first writing contest when I was only thirteen. This was a prelude to God's plan to use writing in a big way in my life. My first book was published (by a real publisher) when I was only twenty and still in college. So don't overlook the things God is doing in your life, and don't assume you are too young to make a big difference.

Talking It Out

Write out a prayer to the Lord explaining areas where you are doubtful or confused. Ask Him to make things clear to you and to reveal Himself to you in the process. If you have specific questions concerning His will for your future (where to go to college, who to invite to camp, and so on), write those questions out now and trust that God will answer them in His timing.

Writing It Down

Take a few moments and reflect on something new you learned about God, His Word, or yourself during this week's lesson.

Setting a Higher Standard

Name one goal that will help you figure out what your role to play in God's story is or something that will get you out there fulfilling that role as soon as possible. Maybe your goal is to find three people to help you review some of your answers. Perhaps you think you might be called to foreign missions, so one of your goals should be to go on a short-term mission trip in the next year.

week six

AN ETERNAL LEGACY

One of the twenty-four elders said to me, "Stop weeping! Look, the Lion of the tribe of Judah, the heir to David's throne, has conquered. He is worthy to open the scroll and break its seven seals."

— REVELATION 5:5 (NLT)

HAVE YOU EVER CHEATED AND read the end of a story before you read its beginning? I know I have. That may be how you feel about reading Leah's story. Before picking up this Bible study, you probably knew that Jesus Christ came to save mankind from sin, but it was less likely that you knew the role Leah played in His coming. God gives each of us a role to play in His story — He doesn't need us, but He chooses to include us even though we are unworthy.

Last week we learned that Leah probably had no idea of the legacy she would leave through her son Judah. Considering you probably aren't a mother at this point in your life, the legacy you are leaving may be even harder for you to figure out. But even if you don't realize it, you are still leaving a legacy.

le•ga•cy: anything handed down from the past

THINKING IT THROUGH

1. List three things that have been handed down to you from
   family members or close friends that can be considered
   part of their legacies. These can be physical items, like your
   grandmother's wedding band, or characteristics or habits, like
   having a daily quiet time.

   a. being a Christian - (living for Christ)
   b. keepsakes from my Grandma
   c.

2. How have these pieces of other people shaped who you are as
   a person?

   helped me to walk w/ Christ

3. List three things you have passed on to someone else (such
   as a younger sibling or a friend who moved away).

   a. toys (from my childhood) to my kids
   b. scripture memorization
   c.

4. How did those pieces of you affect the people you gave
   them to?

   they were happy

5. In your own words, what is a legacy and why is it so
   important?

   something lasting

WHERE A LEGACY BEGINS

Earlier in our study, we noted that Leah's attitude toward Judah's birth was different from her attitude toward that of her other sons. With her first three sons, her focus was on whether or not Jacob would love her as a result. With Judah she loudly proclaimed, "This time I'll praise GOD" (Genesis 29:35). There was something different about Leah's attitude toward Judah from the very beginning, so it is no surprise that he was the son from whom her lasting legacy sprang.

Since legacies can be both good and bad, they don't always begin with the making of *wise* choices. Our legacies do, however, begin at the start of our lives and the start of each day with every choice we make. Each day we can have a fresh start to change what we need to change, and like Leah we can begin praising God where we once tried to manipulate others. Every morning you have the choice to continue the legacy you have already been leaving or to alter it according to what you want it to be.

Here are some verses worth memorizing as you decide to start leaving a legacy of praise like Leah did. Choose the one that stands out to you the most.

> Surprise us with love at daybreak;
>   then we'll skip and dance all the day long. (Psalm 90:14)
>
> Let me hear of your unfailing love to me in the morning,
>   for I am trusting you.
> Show me where to walk,
>   for I have come to you in prayer. (Psalm 143:8, NLT)
>
> It is good to proclaim your unfailing love in the morning,
>   your faithfulness in the evening. (Psalm 92:2, NLT)

LEGACIES AREN'T ALWAYS PERFECT

Although we have a great responsibility to make wise choices as we seek to leave God-honoring legacies, we can be relieved to know we don't have to be perfect for God to use us. Judah, and his lineage, was Leah's greatest legacy. But even Judah, the son of praise, was flawed.

Read the following passage, Genesis 38. Note of caution: This is very mature material, but it is important to know. If what you read troubles you, make sure you discuss it with a trusted youth leader or parent.

About that time, Judah separated from his brothers and hooked up with a man in Adullam named Hirah. While there, Judah met the daughter of a Canaanite named Shua. He married her, they went to bed, she became pregnant and had a son named Er. She got pregnant again and had a son named Onan. She had still another son; she named this one Shelah. They were living at Kezib when she had him.

Judah got a wife for Er, his firstborn. Her name was Tamar. But Judah's firstborn, Er, grievously offended GOD and GOD took his life.

So Judah told Onan, "Go and sleep with your brother's widow; it's the duty of a brother-in-law to keep your brother's line alive." But Onan knew that the child wouldn't be his, so whenever he slept with his brother's widow he spilled his semen on the ground so he wouldn't produce a child for his brother. GOD was much offended by what he did and also took his life.

So Judah stepped in and told his daughter-in-law Tamar, "Live as a widow at home with your father until my son Shelah grows up." He was worried that Shelah would also end up dead, just like his brothers. So Tamar went to live with her father.

Time passed. Judah's wife, Shua's daughter, died. When the time of mourning was over, Judah with his friend Hirah of Adullam went to Timnah for the sheep shearing.

Tamar was told, "Your father-in-law has gone to Timnah to shear his sheep." She took off her widow's clothes, put on a veil to disguise herself, and sat at the entrance to Enaim which is on the road to Timnah. She realized by now that even though Shelah was grown up, she wasn't going to be married to him.

Judah saw her and assumed she was a prostitute since she had veiled her face. He left the road and went over to her. He said, "Let me sleep with you." He had no idea that she was his daughter-in-law.

She said, "What will you pay me?"

"I'll send you," he said, "a kid goat from the flock."

She said, "Not unless you give me a pledge until you send it."

"So what would you want in the way of a pledge?"

She said, "Your personal seal-and-cord and the staff you carry."

He handed them over to her and slept with her. And she got pregnant.

She then left and went home. She removed her veil and put her widow's clothes back on.

Judah sent the kid goat by his friend from Adullam to recover the pledge from the woman. But he couldn't find her. He asked the men of that place, "Where's the prostitute that used to sit by the road here near Enaim?"

They said, "There's never been a prostitute here."

He went back to Judah and said, "I couldn't find her. The men there said there never has been a prostitute there."

Judah said, "Let her have it then. If we keep looking, everyone will be poking fun at us. I kept my part of the bargain — I sent the kid goat but you couldn't find her."

Three months or so later, Judah was told, "Your daughter-in-law has been playing the whore — and now she's a pregnant whore."

Judah yelled, "Get her out here. Burn her up!"

As they brought her out, she sent a message to her father-in-law, "I'm pregnant by the man who owns these things. Identify them, please. Who's the owner of the seal-and-cord and the staff?"

Judah saw they were his. He said, "She's in the right; I'm in the wrong — I wouldn't let her marry my son Shelah." He never slept with her again.

When her time came to give birth, it turned out that there were twins in her womb. As she was giving birth, one put his hand out; the midwife tied a red thread on his hand, saying, "This one came first." But then he pulled it back and his brother came out. She said, "Oh! A breakout!" So she named him Perez (Breakout). Then his brother came out with the red thread on his hand. They named him Zerah (Bright).

6. Was Judah the kind of person you'd expect to leave a God-honoring legacy? Explain your answer.

7. Where did Judah first go wrong? (Hint: There was another mistake before the huge blunder he made by sleeping with Tamar.)

8. Read the lineage of Jesus Christ in Matthew 1:3. Explain the significance of the lineage of the King of kings coming through Perez.

9. How does it make you feel to know that God doesn't expect you to be perfect?

So what do we do? Keep on sinning so God can keep on forgiving? I should hope not! (Romans 6:1)

10. Consider the above verse. Where is the balance between not having to be perfect and using God's grace as an excuse to sin?

11. Describe a situation in your life where you have not been perfect. Have you been able to be repentant for your behavior without constantly hanging your head in shame? Talk about why you have or haven't.

grace: mercy, clemency, or pardon

12. Define *grace* in your own words.

13. What role did God's grace play in the legacies of Leah and Judah?

LEGACIES, INHERITANCES, AND LINEAGES

We also pray that you will be strengthened with [God's] glorious power so that you will have all the patience and endurance you need. May you be filled with joy, always thanking the Father, who has enabled you to share the inheritance that belongs to God's holy people, who live in the light. For he has rescued us from the one who rules in the kingdom of darkness, and he has brought us into the Kingdom of his dear Son. (Colossians 1:11-13, NLT)

As Christians we have a great spiritual inheritance: We are God's children, and we have access to the kingdom of God through Jesus Christ. Because of Christ's death and resurrection, we instantly get to step into His legacy and reap the benefits. We are forgiven and washed clean. God now sees us as pure and spotless. We have inherited eternal life.

14. The legacy of Christ is reflected in the fact that we are called Christians. What does it mean to you personally to bear the name of Christ?

15. Think of your family name (commonly referred to as your last name). What does having that name represent for you?

16. Do you feel any specific pressure or obligations because you are associated with your family name? Explain. (For instance, maybe you have the same teacher one of your siblings had and he or she always associates you with that sibling. Perhaps you have a well-known parent whose shoes you feel you need to fill.)

17. Do you feel any pressures or obligations because you refer to yourself as a Christian? Explain.

Maybe you come from a family where not much is expected of you. Leah and Judah did too. Leah wasn't the chosen wife, and Judah most certainly wasn't his father's favorite. And we can only imagine what life was like for Perez, the son of Judah's embarrassing mistake.

18. Why do you think God chose to use people like Leah, Judah, Tamar, and Perez to carry out the lineage of the Messiah?

THE LEAH SISTERHOOD

19. Matthew mentions three women besides Leah and Tamar in the lineage of the Messiah. Read the following passages about these women and answer the questions about them.

Rahab (Joshua 2:1–24)

a. What was Rahab's occupation?

b. What was her character like?

c. Why do you think she was so willing to help God's people?

d. What did Rahab have to offer God in terms of being someone He would want in the lineage of His Son?

e. Why do you think God chose to include Rahab in the lineage of Christ?

Ruth (Ruth 1–4)

a. What kind of woman was Ruth?

b. Who did Ruth worship at the beginning of the book of Ruth?

c. Was Ruth a Jew — one of God's chosen people? Why did that matter?

d. What did Ruth have to offer God in terms of being someone He would want in the lineage of His Son?

e. Why do you think God chose to include Ruth in the lineage of Christ?

Mary (Luke 1)

a. Mary was a teenager. What kind of girl was she?

b. Describe Mary's response to the angel.

c. What did someone like Mary have to offer God?

d. Why do you think God chose to include someone like Mary in the lineage of Jesus Christ?

Sometimes family members have things in common. Other times they are as different as night and day. Just think of your own family!

20. Make a list of the similarities and differences between Leah and the other women in the lineage of Christ.

Similarities:	Differences:
a.	a.
b.	b.
c.	c.
d.	d.
e.	e.
f.	f.
g.	g.

21. Which of these women do you relate to most? Why?

POP QUIZ

Just to make sure you have been paying attention to what you've been reading, here's a little quiz to test your knowledge! Match the name of the woman below to her description.[2]

1. Mary	a. Not in the lineage of the Messiah
2. Leah	b. Fooled her father-in-law into sleeping with her
3. Tamar	c. Was once a pagan worshiper
4. Ruth	d. Her husband was tricked into marrying her
5. Rahab	e. A teenage virgin in a small town
6. Rachel	f. A prostitute by trade

BEYOND DREAMING

In the end, the women in Christ's lineage left legacies that were far greater than they would have ever dared to hope or imagine for themselves. God desires to do the same thing for us.

> God can do anything, you know — far more than you could ever imagine or guess or request in your wildest dreams! He does it not by pushing us around but by working within us, his Spirit deeply and gently within us. (Ephesians 3:20)

22. What does this verse mean to you personally?

---

2. Correct answers: 1. e, 2. d, 3. b, 4. c, 5. f, 6. a

23. List your three wildest dreams.

    a.

    b.

    c.

24. Imagine God doing something even greater than those three
    things. How does that thought make you feel?

25. What legacy do you hope to leave to your school and youth
    group once you have graduated?

26. If your life were suddenly cut short, what would you want said about you at your funeral?

27. How can you take the necessary steps to make sure that was said?

28. When you think about the legacy you want to leave behind, is it centered on who you are as a person or on what you've accomplished? Explain.

LEAH'S UNLIKELY LEGACY

Our study of Leah's life and legacy is drawing to a close. We have walked through the pages of Scripture with her from the very beginning, when she was just the sister with nice eyes and not much else to offer, all the way to the life of Christ and her role in His lineage. Hers is a remarkable story, one we shouldn't be quick to forget.

29. Make a list of six things you learned throughout the course of this study. Try to think of one point from each week.

    a.

    b.

    c.

    d.

    e.

    f.

30. How has Leah's story influenced your own in the last six weeks?

31. What can you learn from her mistakes?

32. What hope does her story offer you?

Talking It Out

God delights in answering the heart cries of His children. Through Leah's life we learned that He sees our fears and insecurities and He delights in helping us overcome them. As we end our study on Leah, write out your own prayer to God expressing any fears, hesitations, hopes, or dreams you have concerning your own legacy. He'll be delighted to hear from you!

Writing It Down

Before we conclude this study, take a few moments to journal your thoughts on all you have taken in during these last six weeks. Make sure to note the things that challenged you, inspired you, and convicted you. You might want to flip back through the book and read through some of your previous journal entries, goals, and prayers. This will help you see how far you have come in six weeks and might give you a clearer idea of the direction you want to go.

Setting a Higher Standard

By now you should be fully aware that God has a destiny and legacy for you beyond your wildest imaginings. Perhaps you have even gained some key insights into exactly what that might look like for you. List one goal — an area where you want to actively pursue change — in order to be better equipped for what God has for you. Make sure you write today's date next to your goal so you can look back and measure your progress a few months from now.

note to leaders

HOW TO USE THIS BIBLE STUDY IN A SMALL GROUP

WHETHER YOU ARE A VETERAN small-group leader or a rookie taking the field for the first time, it's important that you outline for your group what is expected of them. To help you think through how you want to do things, I offer you six steps I always take when facilitating a small group. You know your group of girls best, so pick and choose from my suggestions what will work for them. But more than anything else, have fun as you lead them through God's Word — and Leah's story — together.

1. At your very first session together, it is important that you go over the rules of confidentiality that you want your group to adhere to. During the course of your time together, some girls in the group may open up about struggles they are facing or painful experiences from their past. It is your job as the group leader to make sure your girls know that things shared with

the group must stay within the group and should not be discussed outside your regular meetings.

2. Since girls have a tendency to talk — a lot — and sometimes get off track, you will need to establish a set length of time for the discussion portion of your group meetings. Some groups may have only half an hour, while others may be able to devote an entire hour. No matter what you decide, be consistent. This will help keep girls engaged and on course. You can also use it as a tool when things get off topic by saying something like, "While this is all good stuff you are talking about, we have only thirty minutes to discuss this week's lesson. So let's save all of these other conversations until after the meeting is over."

3. In your group you will have a variety of personality types. Even if all of the girls are friends outside the group, you will still notice that some of them talk more than others. To keep the group balanced and in order to make everyone feel included, monitor how much one person shares and make note of those who don't seem to open up at all. Try to encourage everyone to talk at least once during group time.

4. I have found that opening each week with an icebreaker question or game puts everyone at ease and gets some of the nervous energy out before actual group discussion begins. Having girls share embarrassing moments, favorite ice cream flavors, or middle names can be a good way to get to know the girls in your group while getting everyone settled in.

5. On average, each week in this Bible study has close to thirty questions for the girls to answer on their own before you meet. Because you will not have time to go over all of their answers in your group time, it will be best for you to go through each lesson before you meet and select five to seven questions you would like your girls to discuss. The first five questions in each week's lesson aren't always the most thought-provoking, so look over all of the questions and see which ones your girls

need to give special thought to. Start your discussion with those.

6. Every time I lead a small group, I like to encourage the girls to be thinking about each other outside the group. This helps them strengthen their relationships with each other and build trust. I hand out 3x5 cards at the end of every group meeting and have the girls write their name and e-mail address or phone number on the top line, and several prayer requests on the lines below. Then I collect all of the cards and let the girls pick a card from a basket. They are responsible for praying for the person they picked and contacting her to encourage her sometime during the week. In all of the groups I have led, girls always list this as one of their favorite parts of the study. Feel free to use your own version of this.

Have a great time with your group!
Shannon

ABOUT THE AUTHOR

TWENTYSOMETHING AUTHOR SHANNON PRIMICERIO resides in Southern California with her husband, Michael. The Primicerios are a fun-loving couple who enjoy watching baseball, playing Bocce ball, flying kites, and hanging out at the beach.

Shannon has a BA in journalism and a minor in biblical studies from Biola University. She was the recipient of the North County *Times* "Excellence in Writing" award in 2000 and the San Diego Christian Writers Guild "Nancy Bayless Award for Excellence in Writing" in 2003.

She has been interviewed on radio and television programs across the nation and was recently featured in such media outlets as PBS's *Religion and Ethics Newsweekly*, *The Harvest Show*, and *TIME* magazine.

Shannon's ministry spans the globe, as her books are available in several languages. Her books include *The Divine Dance, God Called a Girl*, the BEING A GIRL . . . series, and *Life. Now.* (the last of which she cowrote with Michael).

She also serves as a mentor to young authors through the Jerry B. Jenkins Christian Writers Guild. Her articles have appeared in *Marriage Partnership* and *BRIO* magazines.

To learn more about Shannon, please visit www.beingagirlbooks .com. You can also contact her via e-mail at shannon@beingagirlbooks .com.

TWO MORE EXCITING STUDIES FOR TEEN GIRLS!

Author Shannon Primicerio takes a fresh approach to devotional studies by leading you through the lives of three very different women of the Bible: Hagar, Leah, and Miriam. Throughout the TRUELIFE BIBLE STUDIES series, you'll explore each woman's relationship with God, connect with core issues, and discover relevant lessons that can apply to your lives today.

Hagar

ISBN-13: 978-1-60006-113-4
ISBN-10: 1-60006-113-3

While Sarah was given a special promise by God, Hagar and her son were still very much a part of God's plan. This study shows us that no matter how others treat us, we are still loved by God.

Miriam

ISBN-13: 978-1-60006-114-1
ISBN-10: 1-60006-114-1

Although she was often overshadowed by her more famous brothers, Moses and Aaron, courageous leader Miriam played a vital role in the Hebrews' delivery from Egypt.

THINK

NAVPRESS
BRINGING TRUTH TO LIFE
www.navpress.com

To order copies, visit your local Christian bookstore, call NavPress at 1-800-366-7788, or log on to www.navpress.com.
To locate a Christian bookstore near you, call 1-800-991-7747.